Get Past
driving
test
Nerves

GET PAST DRIVING TEST NERVES

Summersdale Publishers Ltd
46 West Street
Chichester
West Sussex
PO19 1RP
UK

www.summersdale.com

Printed and bound in Great Britain

ISBN: 978-1-84024-673-5

This book is dedicated to my daughter Carman

About the author

Lorna Cordwell is a therapist and has her private practice in Harley Street, London. She works with clients on a variety of issues and specialises in relaxation work and hypnosis. Many of her clients want to overcome anxiety and fear in certain situations. The driving test is one such situation. She has worked, with positive results, with people who have failed their test several times and are at the stage of believing that they will never pass.

Like millions of others, she is an ordinary driver who took her driving test twice. The first time, aged 18, her nerves simply failed her on the day. Several years later, on her second attempt, she used relaxation and hypnosis as an aid and surprised herself by not only feeling calm and confident throughout the entire test, but actually liking the experience too.

Trained in Psychology at the prestigious London School of Economics (University of London) and at the National College of Hypnosis and Psychotherapy, she has worked as a therapist since 1987. She is a member of the United Kingdom Council for Psychotherapy, the British Association of Counsellors and Psychotherapists and the National Register of Hypnotherapists and Psychotherapists.

This is Lorna's first book. She lives in London.

Contents

Introduction

Congratulations on making your decision to become a driver and to join the 32 million people in the UK who hold a full driving licence. Driving your own car will give you a sense of freedom and self-control that can open many new possibilities for you.

Your next step is to pass your driving test. Your reading this book may mean that you will soon be taking the test for the first time, or perhaps you have already taken the test and need to retake it. Having picked up this book, you are doubtless expecting your test to be a daunting experience.

Nowadays, the majority of people learn to drive with a qualified instructor, take a course of lessons and read instruction books available. Surprisingly, the driving test pass rate is still only around 44 per cent.

Why do so many still fail? Leaving aside those who are simply not ready, most people fail on the day because of nerves.

Many of us have stories, or have heard stories, of tests where 'I went to pieces', or 'I just couldn't do anything right even though I can drive perfectly.'

Taking a driving test ranks as one of the most stressful experiences that we have in our lifetimes.

It is different from taking exams at school where we have a chance to sit and work at our own pace, and often it is the first time that we have taken a practical exam.

In addition, you know that your driving examiner is not there to help you to calm your nerves. They will not do anything deliberately to make you feel nervous, but their mere presence can have an unsettling effect.

What happens to you then? You hope that you can stay focused, and calm and confident. Feeling this way lets you concentrate on what you are doing. You can use all the skills that you have perfected in your driving lessons, and then your examiner tells you that you have passed the test.

Alternatively, what happens is that you feel a rush of nerves, you lose concentration, you begin to make mistakes, and then fail the test.

I have written this book to help you pass your driving test by feeling less nervous when you take it. It is not an instruction manual on how to drive, and I am not a driving expert. I am an ordinary driver with ordinary driving experience. After taking my driving test twice, I have held a driving licence for around 20 years; I have driven on all kinds of roads in all kinds of conditions and encountered a number of different driving

situations. I am just like the millions of other drivers in the UK.

My expertise in helping you is in a different area; I am a therapist, and I can help you to overcome feelings of anxiety, fear, or nervousness – both before and during your driving test.

This book will help you to take control. It explains what your nerves are, why they occur, and what you can do to calm them when you need to. It will help you to prepare emotionally for your driving test, and to take the test feeling calm and confident. What this book cannot do is teach you to drive. You need a driving instructor to do this for you.

Using the simple and easy-to-follow exercises and methods described, you will gain greater self-control during your test. The sooner you start using the exercises, the stronger their effects will be.

For those who have failed a test, put the experience behind you and see your previous test as a dress rehearsal. This will help you to prepare for the next one.

I suggest you read this book from cover to cover to understand its contents. Then, start the book again and work with it. The later chapters contain exercises. Aim to start these around three or four weeks before your test.

For the main exercises, you will need some form of recorder that you can use to record your voice. The quality just needs to be good enough for you to hear the words clearly when you play the recording back to yourself through headphones or speakers. If this is not possible, you will need to get help from a willing friend or relative to read the exercises to you.

Once you have prepared the exercises, using them is a relaxing and pleasant experience. On the day of your driving test, the exercises will help you to respond in a calmer and more focused manner, and that, after all, is what counts.

Chapter 1

So you want to pass your test?

Some of us sail through new situations. We relax into new challenges and they simply go well for us. Most of us take a little bit of extra time. Some situations are more of a challenge than others, and the driving test tends to be one such challenge.

TIP

Remember: challenges create anticipation, which can be helpful. They make us prepare properly and get us working at our best.

Most people feel some level of anticipation about taking the driving test. The aim is to keep your anticipation levels low and channel your nervous feelings into positive energy. We don't want the anticipation to become too strong, because then we experience a surge of nervous feelings that make us feel out of control.

Your expectations

How we expect to feel has a big impact on how we actually feel. Expectations about the driving test can be a double-edged sword. First, we expect nerves because we always feel nervous in new situations. Is this you?

'I don't like doing new things.'

'I don't like being put on the spot and having to do something.'

'I don't like people watching me do things.'

'I'm not good at challenges.'

The other side of this comes from stories that we hear from friends, family and colleagues about

how difficult the driving test is. These stories create even stronger negative expectations, such as:

'If he failed, I am bound to.'

'Oh, now I know she passed first time, I simply have to.'

'Gosh, his examiner sounds awful, I couldn't cope with that.'

'It's all too difficult, I can never do this.'

'So many people fail, I'll definitely fail.'

How nerves start

General beliefs within society, anecdotes and stories of others' mishaps all condition us to feel nervous about the driving test.

Our expectation of feeling nervous starts long before we have even thought about learning to drive. Don't worry, we can change our expectations so that we feel less anticipation. Once we learn how to reduce this, we can stop ourselves from being affected in negative ways.

Nerves can have all kinds of detrimental effects on us, such as:

- ✓ Sleeping badly
- ✓ Becoming irritable easily
- ✓ Forgetting to do important things
- ✓ Not being able to drive as well as we could previously

When we are driving during the test, nerves can:

- ✓ Affect our level of concentration
- ✓ Make us appear over-confident
- ✓ Make us rather reckless
- ✓ Make us too hesitant
- ✓ Alter our perception of distances or speeds
- ✓ Make us over-talkative
- ✓ Make us appear not to be paying attention at all
- ✓ Make us forgetful
- ✓ Have physical effects such as making us weak and shaky

What are nerves?

The correct term for nerves is anxiety. Anxiety is a group of uncomfortable thoughts, feelings and

SO YOU WANT TO PASS YOUR TEST?

physical sensations that we experience when something frightens or otherwise upsets us. Anxiety can happen very quickly, or it can build over time. Here is the psychological definition of anxiety:

Anxiety is a physical response to a perceived threat.

We all feel anxiety. The feelings are a natural response that happens automatically. They are part of our biological make-up as human beings.

Why do we have anxiety?

Anxiety exists to protect us. The feelings are an automatic way that we have of helping ourselves in threatening situations. However, they happen to us in quite a crude way, and in psychological terms we call this the 'Fight or Flight' response.

The physical feelings of anxiety

The 'Fight or Flight' response produces a number of very noticeable changes in our body. Have a

look at the list below and see if you can remember
feeling any of these:

- ✓ Heart beating faster
- ✓ Pains in chest
- ✓ Shortness of breath
- ✓ Arms and legs feeling weak or shaky
- ✓ Sweating
- ✓ Stomach churning
- ✓ Feeling nauseous or vomiting
- ✓ Going very pale
- ✓ Feeling faint
- ✓ Unable to focus or concentrate

When the feelings start, they are very noticeable,
which makes us feel out of control. Then, we
become anxious about having the feelings and
the intensity increases. We start focusing on them,
losing our concentration, and we are in a vicious
cycle. Why does this have to happen? Believe it
or not, the 'Fight or Flight' response does have a
positive side, but only in extreme circumstances.

The positive side to the 'Fight or Flight' response

People who have been in life-threatening situations
often look back on what happened and wonder

how they ever did what they did to ensure they survived. What happened was that a whole group of automatic responses kicked in before they even realised.

These responses allowed them to be stronger and faster than they ever believed they could be. The body prepared itself automatically. Let us go back to our list and examine what is really happening:

Heart beating faster/ pains in chest
Our heart starts to pump our blood around our system much faster so that all our vital organs are ready to work faster.

Shortness of breath
Our breathing rate increases so that we can move faster.

Arms and legs feeling weak or shaky/ sweating/ feeling faint
Our bodies release a surge of adrenalin, which allows our muscles to work much more effectively.

Stomach churning/ feeling nauseous or vomiting/ going very pale
Blood moves to parts of our bodies that need it most, our vital organs and our muscles, and

moves away from other parts of our bodies that are in less need of it: our stomachs for example, where either the digestive process is put on hold, or we eliminate the contents, making us lighter and able to move even faster.

Unable to focus or concentrate
While all this is going on, our minds are automatically planning escape routes, or defences.

So how is the 'Fight or Flight' response useful to me?

TIP

> The key to overcoming nerves is to stop perceiving the test as a threat.

The 'Fight or Flight' response is not useful to you in your driving test, but it is useful for you to know what the response is and why it happens. If it happens on your test, then this is because you are expecting the test to be a threatening experience. To prevent it happening you need to change the way you feel about the test. Return to the definition of anxiety: anxiety is a physical response to a perceived threat. Change that perception and you will react differently.

It all depends on what we see as a threat.

If we perceive it this way, then almost anything can become a threat.

Phobias are a common way of perceiving something as a threat.

For example, thousands of people regularly travel on the underground; they find it the quickest, most convenient and most economical way to travel. They do it comfortably and automatically without even thinking.

For some people, however, the idea of travelling by tube train, or travelling on an escalator, is a frightening experience. Their perception of it is that it is threatening.

They either avoid travelling this way, or will experience the 'Fight or Flight' response if they attempt to.

How anxiety can create a negative outcome

Anxiety creates negative thoughts as well as physical reactions and negative thoughts heighten anxiety which can send our minds spiralling to thoughts of doom and gloom. Anxiety means that we see the worst in a situation and the worst outcome.

ow many of us can apparently
...re in this way. We start telling
...s like this:

'...eel dreadful on the day.'

'I know I'm not going to pass.'

'I know I won't be able to do my bay parking.'

'Everyone will laugh at me if I fail.'

'I'll never be a driver.'

Just suppose you could tell yourself the opposite:

'I know I'll feel great on the day. I'm prepared and feeling fit and strong.'

'I know I'm going to pass because I've imagined myself doing it.'

'I know I can do the bay parking because I've been doing it well already.'

'Everyone will be so happy for me because I have passed.'

'I'll be a driver really soon now.'

> **TIP**
>
> A positive outcome is just as likely as a negative one: tell yourself that the test will go well.

Well, why can't you? This positive result is just as possible and relevant as anything negative that you might be telling yourself.

Observe your own thoughts and notice whether you are channelling them in this negative direction. Noticing it happening is the first step to stopping it. If it is happening, tell yourself to stop. Now, tell yourself that it is just as likely that you will be the proud owner of a full driving licence soon. Does this feel better? Of course it does. So why give yourself a hard time?

Chapter 2

The capacity of your mind

What we do when we feel threatened

> **TIP**
>
> You do not need to be aware of everything to be in control.

When we feel anxiety, we try to control everything by thinking about everything. When we do this, we usually make things worse for ourselves.

This is because we don't necessarily control things well by thinking about them. This might

seem like a strange statement to you, but it is true. It is important for you to know that you do not have to consciously control everything. In this chapter, I will explain why. When you can learn to let go of consciously trying to control your driving, then you will be a much more relaxed and confident driver.

When you make the decision to learn to drive, you will be receiving 'helpful' tips and advice in all manner of ways. Your driving instructor, friends, relatives and instruction books will tell you the best way to do things. You might notice that it all seems very complicated. You might be getting anxious about all this complication, thinking that you will never be able to remember all this on the day. You're right.

When your driving instructor is teaching you, they are giving you practical tips that you practise. This is the best way to learn. Much of what you are doing is a subconscious process. Let me explain what this means.

Why it is OK to relax and let go

As a therapist, I work with a model of our mind that we call the subconscious. Let me clarify from the beginning that the subconscious mind is

nothing to do with being asleep, or concussed, or unaware in the simple sense. Your subconscious is your total mind capacity. It is all of it. As your mind is working, you are only ever aware of a tiny part of what is happening. We believe that this tiny part is about seven different bits of information at any one time. This information is in our conscious awareness. Everything else is still all there, as memories and processes in the subconscious part of our mind. It is all ready to be accessed at any time, as it is needed. You don't need to be aware of everything in order for it to happen. Your subconscious mind continues to work on your behalf in many ways, whether you are aware of this or not. When you are taking your driving test, you will not have to consciously do everything, because your subconscious mind will be doing a lot for you anyway.

Think about your mind as being like the most complex computer. You have thousands of files and programs stored on your hard drive, but you only have a few files open at any one time. If you tried to open every file that was stored and to read them all at once, your computer would not be able to cope and neither would you.

You know that the hard drive of your computer continues to work outside of your awareness,

reprocessing the information as you are w
on individual files.

Your mind opens and closes those indiv.
files, as you need them, in an ever-changing
process that you do not need to think about.

As soon as you realise that you do not have to try
to be in control of everything all the time, because
you already are, you have a key to lessening
anxiety. You don't need to confuse your conscious
awareness with your total subconscious mind.

EXERCISE

Notice the difference between doing
something automatically, or subconsciously,
and being aware of doing it and being
conscious of it. Read the sentence below and
be aware of how you are reading the words
and how the letters go together to form the
words. Notice how the words look and what
they mean:

*I am a very good driver. I have not yet realised
how good I am, but I soon will.*

It takes a long time to consciously read and we do not grasp the meaning of the sentence in the same way. It is not the same as how you are reading this sentence.

The stages of learning a new skill

When we learn we move through four learning stages:

- ✓ Subconscious incompetence
- ✓ Conscious incompetence
- ✓ Conscious competence
- ✓ Subconscious competence

There was a time when you did not even realise that you could not drive. You did not think about driving. This is subconscious incompetence.

When you realise that you are unable to drive, or that you want to learn to drive, you are in the conscious incompetence stage. You are aware that you are unable to do something.

When you start learning to drive, you are in the conscious competence stage. You know that you are driving, but you are aware of changing gear,

when you should be applying the br
on. You are driving consciously.

This stage can be exhausting. It r
lot of mental energy. You need to m
the stage that all good drivers are in, the stage
of subconscious competence. Then, driving
becomes a skill like reading or walking, that
you can use to do other things. Now you can
concentrate on the road, on where you are
going, on why you are going there. Now you are
a good driver.

Allow the stages to happen

Because we learn new things through these
four stages of learning, we do not need to try to
control the process; it will simply happen, as long
as we allow it. The more you try to control it, the
longer it will take.

Tapping into our existing skills

All we are doing when we learn to drive is making
a few minor adjustments to what we already
know. These adjustments involve judgements of
space, distance and speed. We already have very
fine skills of judgement so they just need slight

29

...mendment. These are skills that we have been born with and become finely tuned from an early age.

Your brain is very good at making these judgements. Through a relatively small amount of practice and experience, your brain can easily adjust to feeling that you are as big and as fast as a car, and then you simply make the same good judgements as a driver.

How do I know that I can be a good driver?

Be assured that you will be a good driver because such judgements are easy for you as a human being.

TIP

Remind yourself that if many other people can drive perfectly, so can you.

If these judgements were not easy, and driving did not become an automatic process for us, then it would not be popular. It would be reserved for specialists – like people who are astronauts or brain surgeons. Perhaps we do not all have the capacity to be astronauts or brain surgeons, but the number of people worldwide who regularly drive proves that driving is something that our brain finds easy to do.

Chapter 3

Learning calm

Stopping anxiety by allowing relaxation to happen

To recap on what we have learned so far:

- ✓ Anxiety creates uncomfortable feelings that are difficult to prevent.
- ✓ This only happens if we expect the driving test to be a threatening experience.
- ✓ When we expect this to be the case, we try to control everything.

✓ When we try to control everything, we drive consciously, which is not the best way to drive.

Now you know what is happening, it is time to start changing this so that the reverse happens for you:

✓ On your driving test, you feel calm, relaxed and focused.
✓ This is because you expect the driving test to be fine.
✓ Therefore, you are paying attention when required and not trying to control everything.
✓ You are able to drive subconsciously, giving full awareness to the road and the instructions you are being given.

You can do this in the ways that this book will show you by learning to relax, and by seeing the driving test as a less threatening event. Learning to relax will not only help you to stop the 'Fight or Flight' response being triggered but will also help to let your subconscious processes work much more effectively.

As you work through this book, your subconscious mind will already be taking in the information.

The exercises in this book will work alongside the way your mind works anyway. You do not need to be convinced, or to have an understanding of how your mind functions, to become a relaxed and happy driver. After all, a very low percentage of drivers are psychologists.

Why learning relaxation will lower anxiety

As a therapist, I use hypnosis techniques in much of my work. A major premise of hypnotherapy is that relaxation is the opposite of anxiety. When we feel relaxed, we simply cannot feel anxious.

By relaxed, I do not mean a level of relaxation that means you want to sleep on the back seat of the car. This relaxation is an inner state of calm where you work in tune with those clever subconscious processes.

This inner calm ensures that you can be alert to everything when you are driving. It is a level of mental and emotional relaxation that allows you to do whatever you want to do as well as you can.

Think about riding a bicycle. As soon as you learn to ride it well, there is a relaxed element about it.

When we are learning, we are nervous at first, as we do not feel completely in control of the machine.

We are wobbly and not entirely convinced that we can stay upright for long.

Then, after a short time, we can simply ride the bike. We relax into it and can ride very well. We no longer worry about wobbling and can concentrate fully on where we are going and what route we are taking to get there.

That feeling of relaxation has kicked in. We simply go with the flow. We are relaxed, yet very active at the same time. Our minds are relaxed when our bodies are working.

Relaxation training

Some of the exercises in this book use principles of hypnotherapy, most notably the relaxation and visualisation exercises. Using these principles, you can replace any previous feelings of anxiety with these new feelings of inner calm. Your mind will do this automatically if you give yourself the time and space to let this happen by doing the exercises properly.

Relaxation training and hypnosis are commonly used by actors, sportspeople and various other professionals to ensure that they are at optimum performance level, and remain focused and calm when required.

As a hypnotherapist, I have helped many clients who believed that they would never be able to stand up on stage and sing, or be able to get onto a plane, or be able to drive. The methods outlined in this book are simple and comfortable – and they work!

Let me share a secret. For driving test nerves, I was my own first client. Way back in time at the age of 18, I took my driving test and failed it dismally. The nerves kicked in. I felt shaky and jittery and, no surprise, I failed.

This failure seemed such a huge thing for me at the time. It upset me so much that I did not get behind the wheel of a car again for eight years.

When I eventually decided that I wanted to be driving, I was through the first stages of my postgraduate hypnotherapy training.

I decided to use the methods that I had learned to discover if they could help me pass my driving test. They did and they worked brilliantly.

This driving test was a completely different experience. I was relaxed and calm. I carried out each manoeuvre smoothly and unhurriedly. I was competent and focused. My test seemed to go very quickly. I admit that I almost enjoyed the experience.

I passed the test and I have been driving happily ever since; so have many people that I have helped pass their driving tests. This book will help you to do the same.

Chapter 4

Taking charge

Giving yourself a hard time

There are many different and quite complex ways in which we can perceive the driving test as a threat. These include:

- ✓ Threats to our self-esteem when we are tested and fail
- ✓ Threats to our confidence when we are tested and fail
- ✓ Threats to our sense of competition when we fail something that others have passed

Sometimes, to stop ourselves feeling threatened in these ways, we learn to give ourselves a very hard time. Unfortunately, this often has the reverse effect of making us feel even worse as we pile the pressure on.

We start an internal thought process, telling ourselves things like 'I simply must pass.' By doing this, you are loading more pressure onto yourself and making the threat larger.

Are you telling yourself:

'I must pass this test.'

'I should pass this test.'

'I have to pass this test.'

Stop for a moment, and ask yourself:

'Says who?'

The answer is *you*. By doing this, you are making a rod for your own back as far as your anxiety level is concerned.

Now ask yourself:

'What will happen if I don't pass?'

At this point, it is common for people to ↱
ahead with a whole group of negative thoughts
such as:

'I'll never learn to drive.'

'I'm going to be taking my test again and
again.'

'I'm going to still be freezing at the bus stop
each winter.'

Stop. Now go back and actually answer the
question. Well, what will happen? Most probably,
one of a small number of things:

✓ You will take the test again and fail.
✓ You will decide not to take the test again.
✓ You will take it again and pass.

Nothing about the driving test gives you only
one chance to pass. You can take it as many times
as you like.

TIP

Remind yourself, it is not that you *must*
become a driver: you have *chosen* to become
a driver.

39

driver is a choice. Realise this and
control over your destiny. When you
that you must do something, you lose
give it to some strange external force
that does not exist. Give yourself an easier time.

Stop this rigid thinking and you lessen your anxiety. Rigid thinking is like looking in a mirror and seeing yourself always wagging a finger at yourself. It helps to set triggers in our subconscious minds that make us see the test as a threat, and you do not want that to happen.

EXERCISE

Over the next few days, actively listen to some conversations, and you will hear the words 'must' and 'should' and the phrase 'have to' used much more than necessary:

'You have to eat those vegetables!'

'I must do the ironing now.'

'You should buy those jeans.'

These orders, because that is what they are, make even the smallest thing seem vitally important, as if something terrible would happen if we did not obey. What is so important about those jeans that we 'should' buy them? Nothing much really.

Politicians use these kinds of statements a lot, inducing a fear and then providing us with the solution that only they can offer. Listen to their speeches and you will hear what I mean.

Now that you have amused yourself by noticing these orders in other people's conversations, it is time to notice them in your conversations and thoughts. You may be surprised just how often you use them.

'I have to leave the house by 8 a.m. otherwise I will be late.'

'I must get to bed early.'

'I should go and visit Aunt Matilda.'

If we let ourselves down by not following the commands, we make ourselves even more

anxious. These commands make the idea of going to see Aunt Matilda a worse experience than it probably is.

Replace those commanding words with something much friendlier, such as 'choose', or 'could', or 'want to'. Then, your statements become:

'I want to leave the house by 8 a.m. otherwise I may be late.'

'I choose to go to bed early.'

'I could go and visit Aunt Matilda.'

Notice that these statements have a much kinder, relaxed feel to them. By being kinder, they do not create anxiety, nor do they shock us into feeling guilty, lazy or inadequate in some way.

So tuck commanding words out of the way and add new ones to your vocabulary. Immediately, you will be easing a burden on yourself that you had created.

Why are you taking the driving test? Because you have chosen to take it, you want to take it, and you have decided that you could take it. Does that feel better? Give yourself an easier time. The driving test is a challenge, so ensure that you have yourself as a friend.

Who is teaching you to drive?

Whoever you choose as an instructor when you are learning to drive, it is important that you have a good rapport with them. Good rapport means that you feel comfortable being with them and that you understand what they are explaining to you.

Your instructor does not have to become a lifelong friend, but you will find your lessons easier if you can relax in their company.

Having a good rapport also means that you have mutual respect for each other and that you are able to speak up if you do not understand something, or if you need more practise on a particular manoeuvre.

Good rapport is not about shouting at each other, storming out of the car, or them laughing at you if you make a mistake. For reasons like these, sometimes it is easier to learn from a professional instructor, rather than a friend or relative.

TIP

A good instructor will help you to feel calm, and a bad one will make you feel worse than if you were on your own.

When I first learned to drive, I accepted my father's offer to teach me. The driving relationship was a disaster, and ended quickly and tearfully with me slamming the car door and storming off home.

The reason for this was my father panicking and grabbing the steering wheel from me several times instead of giving me the opportunity to correct my steering for myself. As you can imagine, none of this did anything to nurture my confidence as a driver.

If a family member, partner or friend offers to teach you to drive, think carefully about accepting their offer. Remember who is in control of learning to drive: it is you. You may be the novice, but learning is your choice, so learn in the way that is right for you and make your lessons work for you. If you feel under pressure from your instructor, then change your instructor. Remember: they are working for you.

You may have seen a TV series called *Britain's Worst Driver*. The show often focused on the 'back-seat drivers' who had been 'encouraging' their unfortunate learner friends or partners.

'Back-seat drivers' are those well-meaning individuals who believe that their judgement is

always better than yours, even when it is you behind the wheel rather than them. These individuals find it impossible to give over control.

Is your instructor letting you take control?

A baby wants to learn to feed themselves at some stage. They instinctively choose to go through the learning process; through trial and error, they will learn how to hold the spoon, and how to keep the food on the spoon. There will be messy mistakes to begin with, but soon they will master it for themselves. Mastery means subconscious competence. If the parents do not let their baby make these mistakes, then the baby will never learn. They are not helping their baby, but rather helping themselves by way of a short-term solution.

Can you do this alone?

Are you worried about your test because you have to take it alone? Some of us always want to have someone else around to help us. This is fine when you are taking your driving lessons, but your instructor is only there to help you to refine your own skills, they are not doing the

g for you and they cannot take the test
u.

r instructor's assessment that you are ready
to take your test is based on their experience, and
on the gradual reduction of the amount of advice
that they give you.

Each time you have a driving lesson, you will be
making more of your own judgements. Gradually,
through practice and experience, you are ready
to drive on your own. The process might look
something like this:

Lesson Number	Percentage of advice needed from your instructor
1–5	100 per cent
6–10	75 per cent
11–15	50 per cent
16–20	25 per cent
21–23	10 per cent
24–25	0–1 per cent
Test day	0 per cent

Feeling the confidence to do things on our own is
something that differs from person to person, but
also something that we can improve.

EXERCISE

Think about how much time you spend relying on other people to be around when you are doing things. Are you the sort of person who is often asking a friend to 'come with me' if you are going shopping or on a journey? Or 'can you help me?' if you are doing housework or your homework?

If you are, start doing more on your own. Sometimes, our lack of confidence to do things ourselves can come from messages that we pick up from people around us. Are the people in your life offering you praise and encouragement, or are they holding you back by giving subtle messages that you cannot do things well; by expecting you to do things wrong or by telling you when you have?

Observe if this is happening to you. If it is, then tell yourself that you are stronger than that. The best way to overcome this is to prove to yourself and to others that you can do it. Start small. If someone jokes that you

are untidy, then disprove them and show how tidy you can be. Let yourself feel your sense of achievement.

Spend more time doing some simple tasks on your own, so that you can see and feel just how much you can do. Practise as the days go by, just by deciding that there are now things that you are going to do alone.

Doing things because you want to, when you want to, and how you want to do them is empowering. When you do things alone you do not have to compromise at all. Start to feel your strength and let it encourage you to do even more on your own. Spend quality time with yourself.

As you do this more often you will recognise that you are the best person to make decisions that affect you.

EXERCISE

Think about the personal space that you have at home. Do you have your own room in the house where you live?

If you are sharing with someone else, do you have, or can you find, a space that is all your own? Perhaps you have a study or a garage. Whatever personal space you do have, spend time in it now and ask yourself whether it feels like your space. Is it private to you? Is it personal to you? Is it decorated and furnished to your own taste and reflecting your individual character?

If you do not have a space that is entirely your own, attempt to create it. Spend time in your space where you can feel completely yourself, with your books, your music, photos and so on.

Your own sense of space is important to you. Spending time in it is spending time with you. This helps enormously to improve your confidence.

Read this book and practise the exercises in your personal space. Your space will allow you to concentrate fully on yourself and your plans.

Chapter 5

Getting prepared

Being prepared is a great way of reducing anxiety. Instead of trying to lessen the threat of the driving test by forgetting that it is happening soon, embrace the challenge and be ready. Knowing what to expect helps us to feel comfortable about the future.

Being emotionally and mentally prepared

A very helpful aspect of the driving test is that you know in advance everything that you are

expected to do. This allows you to plan and prepare for every aspect of it.

When was the last time you took an exam in which you had all the questions in advance?

Besides gaining the practical knowledge for your test through regular lessons, you have time to become mentally and emotionally prepared. This will prove to be a winning combination.

It would be impossible for an athlete to win a race unprepared – they need to be physically fit and well trained, but also mentally rehearsed for the race itself, so that they know what to expect on the day.

To encourage your mental preparation, acknowledge the test date as a reality. Now, let us look at different ways to work towards that date to ensure that you give yourself the best possible chance of passing.

Being proactive

Passing the driving test is not actually the challenge. Rather, your challenge to yourself is in your decision to become a driver. Passing the test is your initiation into becoming a driver. This is your choice, and your challenge. Now confirm your choice by discovering what you

...d difficult so that you can find your solutions these difficulties.

EXERCISE

Get some paper and a pen and write a list of what you find most difficult about the test. Write everything that you can think of and be honest with yourself.

Perhaps you have a list that looks something like this:

a) I can't do three-point turns.
   My gear changing is still too jerky.

b) My work/school colleagues will feel sorry for me if I don't pass.
   I do not have the money for more lessons if I do not pass.
   It will be ages before I can get a car if I do not pass.

c) I will be so nervous I won't be able to do anything.

I have broken the above six statements into three different sections:

Section a) contains practical concerns.

Section b) contains examples of negative future pacing.

Section c) contains general feelings of anxiety.

See if you can put the statements on your list into these sections.

Instead of worrying about the section a) statements, you can take immediate steps to overcome these concerns.

Sometimes, to help ourselves feel better, we keep practising what we are good at and avoid things that we can't do well. On the day of the test, we hope that we will not be asked to do the difficult manoeuvres; or we trust to luck that we will do them well. Be proactive and face what you find difficult so that you can overcome it.

53

Your driving instructor will probably know what these problem areas are, but they are not a mind reader. If you are concerned about something, tell them and ask for extra time on these areas. If you think they are not appreciating how you are feeling about a particular manoeuvre, then tell them. Remember: these are your lessons, and this will be your test.

It is self-defeating to tell yourself that you cannot do something. Instead, tell yourself that you are practising the manoeuvres more and soon you will be able to do them, then you will stand a greater chance of doing them well.

When you do them well, remember this and keep remembering it. Remind yourself that you can do them. Soon, the statements in section a) will be coming off your list.

The statements in section b) are examples of the negative spiral of anxious thoughts described earlier. These statements look to the future and imagine the worst outcome. If these three statements were not on the list, we would feel much more positive.

To overcome these types of thoughts, you can positively reason with yourself.

The first statement in section b) says:

'My work/school colleagues will feel sorry for me if I don't pass.'

Well, so what if they do? Is that such a bad thing? Perhaps it is a good thing that they think enough to offer their sympathy. Would you rather they felt happy that you did not pass? You do not expect them to feel depressed on your behalf. Most probably what will happen is that there will be a few minutes of helpful comments and then life will carry on as usual.

Get the idea?

By reasoning, you will recognise that the truth of the original statements is very uncertain and that there are many other more positive possibilities.

If you find this reasoning difficult to do, then ask a friend or family member to work with you on this.

Finally, section c) contains statements of general anxiety that are a result of the statements in sections a) and b). Remove the sections a) and b) statements by practice, discussion and reasoning, and the section c) statements will lessen or disappear completely.

General well-being

> **TIP**
>
> A period of eating a simple well-balanced diet could do wonders for your anxiety levels.

You can concentrate, carry out tasks better and remain calm if you are feeling fit and well. A good level of fitness and well-being is not just physical, but mental and emotional too.

There is now a wide body of research linking diet and exercise to emotional and mental well-being. I recommend you start or maintain a course of multivitamins for a couple of months before you take your test. The correct balance of essential nutrients plays an important role in reducing our overall levels of stress and anxiety.

Generally, a diet containing a wide variety of good nutritious foods will work wonders for your concentration and will help to keep anxiety and stress levels to a minimum. So make some changes to your diet if you think that this would be beneficial. It will not just be your performance on your driving test that improves, but other areas in your life will benefit too.

Try to cut down on sugars and caffeine. Caffeine is contained in coffee, tea and many fizzy drinks. Both sugar and caffeine have the effect of giving you a big boost of nervous energy, which is exactly what you don't want on the day of your driving test – your own adrenaline will already be providing quite enough of that.

The boost of energy that you feel from sugar and caffeine is a false one, which will peak and drop very quickly. The boost can make you feel quite exhausted afterwards so that you feel the need for more sugar or caffeine, and before you know it, you are feeling a constant high.

A much healthier approach is to choose foods that contain complex carbohydrates or natural sugars, which give you a gradual and slow release of energy throughout the day. In this way, you are working at a good, steady and constant level. Fresh fruits, vegetables, pulses, rice and grains are all good sources of these complex carbohydrates and natural sugars. Add more of these to your diet if you can.

A great food to add is porridge. I recommend that you eat a bowl of porridge on the morning of your driving test. Oats, particularly the whole variety, are a very good source of vitamin B, which can directly reduce our levels of stress and anxiety.

Another good reason for you to cut down on caffeine and sugar-rich foods and drinks is that it will improve your chances of having a good night's sleep. Moreover, if you need to drink coffee or tea every day to get you going in the morning, you might not be getting enough sleep.

Get adequate sleep

Getting a good night's sleep will make a big difference to your level of calmness on the day of your driving test. Do not just think about getting a good night's sleep on the night before your test, think about getting a good night's sleep each night for at least a week before your test. That way, you will be well rested, and if you do happen to have poor sleep for one night, you will still feel the benefit from the rest of the week.

If you have difficulty sleeping, the traditional remedy of a hot bath and a warm milky drink before bedtime can really help. The scripts later in this book can also aid sleep if you play them before bedtime.

I would not recommend the use of sleeping tablets or tranquilising medication if you are having difficulty sleeping before your driving test. Many medicines have side effects that include

lack of concentration and drowsiness and they are not suitable to take if you are driving. If you have prescribed medication, you should talk to your doctor about your plans to drive.

It would be unwise to ask your doctor to prescribe medication specifically for driving-test nerves. Any such medication may have the effect of changing your awareness and your concentration and this could be to the extent that you are an unsafe or even an illegal driver.

Check also before taking any over-the-counter medication for common ailments such as colds or hay fever, as some of these medicines have side effects of making you feel drowsy. Do read the label before you take anything.

As for recreational drugs or alcohol before or during your test, do not even think about it.

The advantages of regular exercise

TIP

Remember: a healthy body goes a long way to having a healthy mind, which means you are more likely to be relaxed and less anxious.

Regular exercise can help relieve general anxiety and stress as well as improving your fitness and strength. When you exercise, you release chemicals called endorphins into your bloodstream, chemicals with a 'feel-good factor', which help you to stay relaxed. They affect your overall mood, giving you a general sense of well-being.

Ensuring that you have regular exercise for at least a few weeks before your test will benefit the work that you are doing. Do not overdo it though – you do not want to have to take the test with an injury or muscle stiffness. Some gentle exercise or fun team sports will make you feel much stronger and fitter and ready to take on anything.

Chapter 6

Taking responsibility for passing the test

Often when people have failed a driving test they blame someone or something else.

Blame for not passing the test can fall on:

- ✓ Your driving examiner
- ✓ Your driving instructor
- ✓ Someone or something else upsetting you before the test
- ✓ Someone else on the road doing something you didn't expect
- ✓ You

When people fail their driving test they often blame the driving examiner for not passing them. If you have taken a driving test before and you feel that the examiner was responsible for you failing, then do read this chapter especially carefully. By blaming someone else you are giving your power over to them, which will not help your confidence and calmness.

❯ You and only you are responsible for passing the driving test. By being responsible for passing, you also need to be responsible for failing. *❮*

There are many myths surrounding driving examiners. We can start to see them as figures of authority, as people who have a power to alter the course of our future in just a few minutes. In extreme cases, people perceive them as frightening individuals who somehow get pleasure out of other people's misery.

It is all too easy to blame the examiner for not passing us rather than having to admit to ourselves that we were not good enough on the day. The excuses that the driving examiner 'just had it in for me', 'took an instant dislike to me', 'didn't know what they were talking about', and so on, are often heard from those who have failed their driving test.

TIP

Do not give your power away by blaming others. If you fail, it is only your fault.

These excuses are easy to justify because the decision whether you pass or fail does rest with just one person, not a group, and not with a set of scientific measurements. It is, if you like, just you against them. Blaming them for not passing you does not help you in any positive way at all.

If you failed, it is your fault. Even if another driver created a difficult situation for you, how you responded would have determined whether your instructor thought that you handled it well. By taking responsibility for yourself, you take the power away from the examiner in your mind. By removing their power, you lower your anxiety about them. Start to think about your examiner in a different way from now on.

Your driving examiner

The next time that you are on the road, thank those driving examiners for ensuring that you are as safe as you can be.

The next time you approach a junction, thank the driving examiner who ensured that other drivers know to give way when they reach that junction, rather than crash into you.

The next time you are passing a car at the side of the road, thank the driving examiner who ensured that the waiting driver knows not to blindly pull out without looking to see you approaching.

Driving examiners have not always existed. In the early days, many years went by with very few driving regulations or guidelines, even though the number of cars on the road was growing swiftly.

These days, driving tests are organised by the Driving Standards Agency, which operates around 400 test centres in England, Scotland and Wales on behalf of the Department for Transport, which is a government agency. Driving examiners are civil servants.

The only criterion that the examiner has for passing or failing you is the set standards of driving ability that you are required to achieve. They must be confident that you are ready to be driving on the roads on your own.

The process of applying to become an examiner is a rigorous one, and yes, the examiner does have to take a driving test – one that is quite a lot more

difficult than yours, so they can empathise with how you feel!

Why it is good to have high standards

Many of us have been to foreign countries where the driving test is non-existent, and we can all vouch for how unsafe it feels to be on the road in those countries.

To have roads as safe as ours, it is vital that we have consistent high standards. The skill of the driving examiner is to maintain these high standards. For the driving examiner, there cannot be any exceptions to these standards.

They cannot pass a candidate because they think they were having a bad day and are sure they could drive well enough on any other day.

Let's thank our driving examiners, who do an important job to keep our roads safe. Let's thank them for ensuring that when you do pass, you know that you really are good enough. Driving is a big responsibility.

Your driving examiner does not want to fail you. There is no reward in failing someone. They want to witness the joy of you passing your test, just as we all like things to go well. They will do what they

can to help you feel at ease, but at the end of the day, they cannot pass the test for you, and they cannot alter their judgement if they consider that you are not yet a safe and competent driver.

Your examiner will have the experience to know the difference between being a little nervous because you are taking a test, and being a completely nervous driver. The former type of nerves, they can take into account.

On the day of the test, both you and your driving examiner will have a set of responsibilities. You will be responsible for driving calmly, confidently and safely. In other words, you will be responsible for passing your test.

Your examiner will be responsible for testing your capabilities to drive well and safely and when they tell you that you can do this, you will know that you have really achieved something to a high standard.

Do not make the mistake of taking on their responsibility and questioning or arguing with their judgement. They are a skilled driver with a lot of extra training and experience. If they tell you that you did not complete something well enough then you must believe them.

A positive attitude towards your driving examiner will do a lot to help you feel calmer

about your driving test. So take on board what I have been discussing in this chapter. If you are ready to take responsibility for passing the test, then it's time to proceed with the scripts.

Chapter 7

Working with the scripts

In the second half of this book I have included a series of scripts and exercises for you to use. They will help you to reduce significantly any experience of anxiety that you might be feeling, and they will in turn help you feel much more relaxed about your driving test.

The most important of these is contained in the next chapter. It is a script that you need to listen to and I will explain how you need to do this.

The script is a hypnotherapy script that allows you to make changes comfortably and easily to

the way you have been thinking about the test. The script is entirely safe and comfortable to use, and once prepared is easy to work with. Do take the time to prepare it. This script uses the same principles that I have been applying in my therapy practice with many hundreds of clients. This is your opportunity to use these principles for yourself.

How the script works

Earlier on in this book I talked to you about expectations. If you expect or believe that you will pass your driving test, you are more likely to do so.

One powerful way that our mind believes that a positive result is possible is if we have had experience of this outcome before.

If you have seen yourself pass, you are more likely to believe that you will pass again.

Those of us who have already passed the driving test believe more strongly that we could pass it again.

If you think you will fail, the script will help you to believe otherwise. It works with you at a subconscious level so you do not even have to think about what it is saying too much. Keep in

mind the letting go of conscious control that was previously discussed.

Each time you play the script, you will subconsciously believe more and more that you can take your test in a relaxed, calm and focused way, and that you will drive well and pass the test.

Preparing the script

The script needs to be recorded or read to you, rather than read by you. When listening to the words you need to be able to lie back quietly and undisturbed with your eyes closed. You need to do this as many times as you can before your driving test.

Simply reading the words in this chapter will not have the desired effect. For this reason, you need to make a recording of yourself reading the script. Once the recording is completed, you are free to play the script as often as you like.

How you record the script is entirely up to you. A cassette tape, digital or CD recording will all be equally effective as long as your voice is clear enough.

If you find it impossible to record the script yourself, then you will need to enlist the help of

a friend or relative who will be willing to read the words to you while you relax – do ensure that they realise that they will need to do this regularly.

When to play the script

Once you have your recording, play the script regularly right up to the day of your driving test. Understand that the recording you have made is a basic relaxation script, so it may make you feel drowsy or even fall asleep.

For this reason, it is vital that you *never* play it when you are driving, or in a car where another driver can hear it.

Play the script from beginning to end undisturbed – and when you have allowed yourself enough free time to play it. Do not play it if you know someone is phoning you in five minutes, or the dinner has to be ready in 20 minutes.

Find yourself free time every day to play the script, and always play it through to the end.

If you find the recording makes you fall asleep, don't worry. Your subconscious is still receiving the message. Use the script at bedtime before you go to sleep at night if you wish.

The ideal amount of time to start working with the script is around three weeks before your test.

...t is less than three weeks away, do not
...y time that you can play the script will
...e benefit for you so just start the work
...as you can.

How to play the script

Get into a comfortable position, either sitting or
lying down. Make sure that you are warm and will
be undisturbed by others – unplug the telephone
if you need to.

Now, simply rest and turn on your recording.
Headphones are better than speakers if you can
arrange this.

Close your eyes and listen to the words. Don't
try to pay attention too closely, just listen and
follow the instructions.

If you find yourself drifting off, that's fine. If
you find yourself thinking about other things,
gently bring your awareness back to the
recording.

After listening to your recording, you will feel
calm and relaxed. This is a pleasant feeling and
one to be enjoyed. With today's hectic lifestyles,
it's all too difficult to give ourselves time to relax,
but when we do, we feel enormous benefits from
it. Over time, this type of relaxation can reduce

our blood pressure, and boost our immune system so that we suffer fewer colds and coughs. We also find that we have more energy and can concentrate more effectively.

Recording the script

When recording the script, speak clearly and slowly, emphasising any important words or phrases. Take your time. Leave gaps between the sentences. Imagine that you are reading a bedtime story to a young child. When we are relaxed, we sometimes think more slowly, and it is good that the script is in pace with this relaxation. Use a soothing tone of voice, keeping the words spoken quietly, and not rushed.

Everybody's speech speed is different, but the recorded script is intended to be around 30 minutes long. If your recording lasts only 20 minutes, then you have rushed through this important preparation process, so give yourself another go so that you are doing as much as possible to promote your own relaxation.

EXERCISE

Try reading this test passage. It will help you to establish the right pace of reading before you record your script.

When you are ready, take a glance at the clock and then read aloud the following passage. It should take you around two minutes to do so. If you are reading it in less than two minutes, go back over it until you have slowed down sufficiently.

The dots between words are an indication of gaps to leave when you are speaking. Put emphasis on the words in capitals.

Test passage

'...From THIS MOMENT FORWARD... I know that I AM GETTING BETTER AND BETTER... From this moment forward... I KNOW... that I am MORE CONFIDENT, MORE RELAXED AND MORE CALM whenever I think about my driving test... This is because... I am better prepared... and because I understand better... why I

have been feeling... the way that I have... I know now... that MY THOUGHTS... AND FEELINGS... AND ACTIONS ARE PERFECTLY... WITHIN MY CONTROL... I know... that on the day of my test... I will feel REALLY GOOD, REALLY CALM AND CONFIDENT... I know... that on the day of my test... I will drive REALLY WELL... because I CAN DRIVE REALLY WELL... I know that ON THE DAY OF MY TEST... I WILL BE CONFIDENT... AND CALM because I am already growing my inner calmness... and confidence every day in every way... EVERY DAY... IN EVERY WAY… I AM BECOMING MORE CALM... AND MORE CONFIDENT... and because I am becoming... calmer and more confident... I know that I am able to do so much more.'

Get the idea? Now use the same pace and emphasis of speaking when you are recording the driving test script, nice and clearly.

Chapter 8

The driving test script

'Now... just sitting or lying back with your eyes gently closed... just allow yourself to get into a nice, comfortable position so that you can really relax.

You don't have to do anything at all now... just simply listen and let your mind wander... you don't have to do anything at all except listen to these words.

This is a very pleasant and relaxing feeling. Listening to these words will help you to feel really relaxed.

Now, keeping your eyes closed... just concentrate on your body for a moment... Allow all the

muscles in your body to really, really relax… Take a mental journey through your body now… so that you can allow all the muscles in your body to relax…This is a very comfortable and pleasant feeling… and you can just let it happen… Let it happen in its own time… in your own way.

So… start with your feet and toes now… Concentrate for a moment on your feet and toes … and as you do so allow all the muscles in your feet and your toes to really relax… Let those muscles relax and go soft and stretch out… A very pleasant feeling… Now allow this pleasant feeling of relaxation to move further up your legs… into your ankles and your calves… Let all those muscles really relax… Stretching and softening.

Now take that feeling of deep relaxation… further up into your knees and your thighs… so that all the muscles in your legs are really relaxing… A very pleasant and calming sensation… and as you become more physically relaxed… so you become more mentally relaxed as well… and you can just let your mind wander in its own unique way.

Now move that feeling of relaxation up… into the muscles of your hips, your buttocks and your lower back and stomach… Feel all those muscles

really relaxing… A very pleasant and comfortable feeling… Very pleasant and comfortable.

Now move that feeling of relaxation further up… into the muscles of your middle and upper back, and your chest… Allow those muscles to really stretch out and relax… and as this happens… very naturally… so your breathing can become deeper… and longer… and more relaxed… Let all those muscles really relax.

Now take that feeling of relaxation… into the muscles of your arms and your hands… so that all the muscles in your upper arms, your forearms… your wrists and your hands are really relaxing… A very pleasant and comfortable feeling… Now take that feeling of relaxation into the muscles of your shoulders and your neck… Let those muscles of your shoulders and your neck… really soften, stretch and relax… Very comfortable.

Now take that feeling of relaxation up… from your neck to your chin, your jaw and your head… All the muscles of your face… your mouth… your cheeks… your nose… around your eyes… and your forehead… Really, really relaxing… Now take that feeling of relaxation… to the muscles of your scalp… the top of your head… the back and sides of your head… allowing all those muscles to completely relax… to soften… and really relax…

Now all the muscles in your entire body are relaxed… and this is a very pleasant and comfortable feeling… and you can just lay or sit there… so relaxed… and so comfortable… just listening to these words.

Now that you are feeling much more physically relaxed… so you are feeling more mentally relaxed too… And with this feeling of relaxation… comes a really lovely sense of calm and tranquillity… Calm… Calm… Say the word through your mind… and as you say the word through your mind… so you experience that wonderful feeling of calm and tranquillity.

As you are simply sitting or lying back and relaxing… you can take some time now… to think about your driving test that you are taking very shortly… This is an exciting time… Soon you will be a fully competent… and confident driver… like so many other drivers… Soon you will be able to travel wherever you would like to go… whenever you would like to go there… secure in the knowledge that you… like so many others… can independently travel whenever you wish to… whenever you need to… whenever you would like to.

Imagine now… imagine now that you have passed your test… and you can see yourself,

relaxed and happy... driving your car... Taking yourself on a very pleasant journey... perhaps to visit friends, or to visit a place that you have always loved... See how easy it is to get there... See how easy it is to take whatever luggage you want to take with you... not worried about carrying it, it will simply fit into your car... See yourself, relaxed and happy... a confident and calm driver.

Soon this will be you... Just a short amount of time is between you at this moment... and you being that calm and happy driver... Just a short test exists between you at this moment... and you being a calm and happy driver.

You are preparing well, very well for the test... You know that you are a very good driver... and as each day goes by, this knowledge grows stronger... Your instructor has told you that you are ready to take the driving test... and your instructor knows that this is true... You carry out all the manoeuvres really well... and as each practice session goes by, you become more and more skilled at those manoeuvres... You are keen to practise... keen to hone your skills... and you are spending time each day... preparing mentally and practically for the test.

Now allow yourself to feel really relaxed and calm... as relaxed and as calm as you can

feel… Really grow that feeling of relaxation and calmness… breathe in relaxation and calmness now so that the feeling grows stronger and stronger within you… Now hold that feeling within you… and as you do so… in turn, you feel a very strong feeling of confidence… Now you are feeling confidence… Feel that confidence growing stronger and deeper within you… Feel where confidence sits within your body… As you feel more and more confident… you feel even more relaxed and calm… As you feel more relaxed and calm… so you feel even more confident… and these feelings of calmness… relaxation… and confidence… are growing stronger within you as each day goes by… As they grow stronger… so you will feel more relaxed… and more confident… about everything you do… everything you want to do… everything you need to do… Calm and relaxed and confident.

Now… you see yourself as calm, relaxed and confident… Get a clear picture of yourself in your mind as a calm, relaxed and confident person… See how happy you look… See how confident and bright you look… Now… imagine that the image of yourself that you see… is yourself on the morning of your driving test… feeling calm… relaxed… and confident… See that you have

had a good night's sleep... and that you are well rested... See yourself looking well rested and alert... See yourself looking calm and confident... Now grow this picture stronger... Allow this image of yourself to grow bigger and brighter and stronger... Give depth to this picture... Hear yourself calm... and relaxed... and confident... hear your voice speaking, smoothly, controlled as you listen... See and hear yourself as you prepare for the day ahead... Having something light to eat and drink... dressing in clothes that make you feel confident and feel relaxed... and preparing yourself for the day.

Now... allow this image to move forward in time... See yourself being greeted by your instructor for your pre-test driving lesson... See yourself feeling comfortable and relaxed as you get into the car... and see yourself making... all the necessary adjustments to the mirrors... the seat... seat belt... and steering wheel... so that you feel as comfortable... and relaxed as possible... See how calm... and relaxed... and confident you are... See that you are smiling... ready and looking forward to the day... You know... that soon you will be a driver with a full licence... See yourself... becoming even more confident and calm... the moment that you hold the steering wheel... and

see yourself moving the car smoothly... easily... like the most natural feeling in the world.

Say the word 'calm' through your mind... and feel that wonderful experience of calm... and confidence... growing stronger and stronger within you... as you see yourself driving that car... looking so calm... so confident... and so perfectly in control... See yourself as fully aware and alert to everything that is happening around you... fully alert to the performance of the car... and see yourself feeling the controls of the car... and handling them perfectly.

See yourself... completing all manoeuvres perfectly... and accurately... and driving to the test centre calmly... confidently... and ready.

Now... see yourself arriving at the test centre... and leaving the car to go through necessary details... See yourself checking the position of the car... knowing where you have parked the car... and checking the number plate of your car... See yourself confident... and relaxed... and calm... as you go through the preparations at the test centre and then await your turn.

See yourself in your mind's eye now... happy and relaxed... waiting your turn... Say the word 'calm' through your mind... and experience that wonderful feeling of calm... and confidence...

as you see yourself waiting... See how calm you are... as you wait your turn... Now see that feeling of calmness increasing... as your examiner greets you... and you are ready to begin your test... As you see yourself walk to the car... you can see how in control you are... how focused... and relaxed... and calm you are.

Now... see yourself calm... and relaxed... and confident... as you carry out all the pre-test checks on the car... and follow your examiner's instructions... easily and comfortably.

Now in your mind's eye... see yourself getting into the car with your examiner... and see your level of calmness... and confidence... and control... increase as your hands touch the steering wheel... See yourself ready and willing to begin the test... As you move off smoothly and easily in your mind's eye... you can see that you are perfectly in control... and that the examiner is relaxed next to you... See that you are hardly noticing that he or she is there... except that you are alert to his or her instructions and carrying those instructions out perfectly... Your awareness is focused on the road... reading the road perfectly... obeying all road sign instructions and signals... as the car travels smoothly and easily.

See yourself... calm... controlled... and confident... as the car travels perfectly... always at the correct speed... always in the correct gear... always in the correct lane... and at the correct distance from other vehicles and objects... See how happy and relaxed you look... as you continue on your drive... See yourself automatically checking your mirrors... and blind spots as much as you need to... easily and directly.

See yourself... handling all your manoeuvres well... Carrying out all the instructions that your examiner gives to you... calmly... unrushed... unhesitatingly... easily and directly... See yourself looking perfectly in control... Calculating everything perfectly... and everything happening so smoothly and so easily... See yourself now... going through each manoeuvre in turn... and each one happening easily... comfortably... and perfectly.

See yourself now in your mind's eye... calm... confident... and in control... as the examiner begins to direct you back to the test centre... Surprised at how quickly the time has passed... See yourself in your mind's eye as you pull into the test centre... feeling confident and pleased that the test has gone so well... You know that it has gone well... You feel that it has gone well.

See yourself... in your mind's eye... as you pull into a parking position at the test centre... and safely park the car... See how calm... focused... and confident you are... See how pleased you are... pleased with yourself... and pleased with the result... as the examiner tells you that you have passed the test... See your pleasure... your confidence... as you realise that now you are a full driver... and that you have passed the test confidently... easily and well.

See yourself calm... confident... and joyful... as you greet your instructor with the good news... and see how good you feel... as you travel home knowing... that you are now a full driver... and that you have passed your test... and passed it well... See how strong you feel... how relaxed... and how pleased... Grow that image strong in your mind's eye now... Grow that image stronger... bigger... and brighter... Give depth and colour to that image of yourself... as a confident... calm... controlled driver... with a full driving licence.

Now... allow yourself to hold this image in your mind's eye for a few moments longer... This is what is going to happen for you... Just as you have seen it happen... You know that you will pass your test easily... and calmly... and

confidently… You know this because you have seen it in your mind's eye… You know that you will do this just as you have seen it happen in your mind's eye… Because you know this… you feel confidence now… Confidence in yourself… and confidence in your own ability… You feel so calm now… Calm throughout your entire body… and your entire mind… These feelings of confidence… and calmness are growing stronger… and stronger within you as each day passes… Stronger and stronger… and surer and surer… So strong… and so sure that nothing will eradicate them… More confident… and calm… than you have felt for a long time… and this feeling of confidence… and calm… will grow stronger… and stronger as each day goes by… Allowing yourself to feel so good… so relaxed… and so in control.

Just allow yourself a few more moments of relaxation… In a few moments' time I shall count to three… and as I count… you will become fully awake and fully alert and completely ready to carry on your day… Then… I shall tell you to open your eyes… and you will open your eyes and be ready to carry on your day feeling alert and awake and calm and confident… As you continue listening to these words you know now

that the time is coming very quickly now when you are ready to open your eyes and be fully awake once more, fully back to full conscious awareness now. Beginning to count now... one... two... and three knowing now that you are fully wide awake and open your eyes.'

Chapter 9

General relaxation and confidence script

When you have played your recording of your driving test script a few times you will notice that it makes you feel very good. The relaxation that it helps you to maintain has overall benefits for you as well as benefits specific to your driving test. You will find that you are increasing your overall level of relaxation and calmness, which has positive effects on other areas of your life.

Below is a general relaxation and confidence script. Several of my clients use recordings of similar scripts between hypnotherapy sessions. It

is always good to find time for ourselves when we can simply relax. Playing a recording of this script regularly can be helpful in reducing an overall level of stress.

While you are preparing for your driving test, you can record this script and play it as well as your driving test script if you wish, perhaps alternating them on a daily basis. Of course, once you have passed your driving test, you will have no need to play the driving test script, but you can keep using the script in this chapter.

General relaxation script

'Now… just sitting or lying back with your eyes gently closed… just listening to the sound of my voice… just allow yourself to get into a nice comfortable position so that you can really relax.

You don't have to do anything at all now… just simply listen and let your mind wander.

You don't have to move… although you may if you want to… and you don't have to talk… You don't have to do anything at all except listen to these words.

This is a very pleasant and relaxing feeling… You can just let go and feel really relaxed… Listening to these words will help you to feel really relaxed.

Now… keeping your eyes closed… just focus on your body for a moment… Allow all the muscles in your body to really relax… Take a mental journey through your body now… so that you can allow all the muscles in your body… to really relax… This is a very comfortable and pleasant feeling… and you can just allow yourself… to let it happen… Let it happen in its own time… in your own way.

As you are doing this… just allow yourself now… to begin to focus your attention inwards… so you can just begin to let your mind drift… Drift as in a pleasant daydream… just letting go of your day-to-day concerns… and allowing your mind to drift towards more pleasant thoughts… More relaxed thoughts… more gentle thoughts.

Imagine now… in your mind's eye… that you are standing on a beautiful beach… A really beautiful beach… Give yourself some time now… to really see this beach… and to grow this picture in your mind… Whatever picture comes to mind… allow yourself to grow this picture in your mind… Whatever you find most beautiful about this beach… allow yourself to grow this in your mind's eye… Notice the colour of the sky and if there are any clouds… Allow yourself some time now to look at the sky… noticing how calm

and relaxed… and happy it makes you feel… Now notice the water… its colour… its stillness or movement… and allow yourself to look out across it… as far as you can see… Notice where the sea meets the sky… at the horizon… and how distant and hazy or clear that is.

Feel in your mind's eye… the ground beneath your feet… Whether this is sandy… or rocky… hard or soft… and sense its warmth or coolness… dryness or dampness… and how this feels to you… so good, so relaxing… Feeling now the temperature of the place… its warmth or coolness… whether there is a breeze… or whether the air is warm and still… lazy, serene.

As you feel these sensations… so you notice that this place is so deeply relaxing… so deeply comfortable… and how relaxed and comfortable you are feeling… Take a nice deep breath… and sense any aromas that you can smell… Perhaps the freshness of the air… or the lovely deep smell of the sea… As you notice this… you are feeling even more comfortable and relaxed… It is as if you are breathing in the calmness… and relaxation… of this lovely place with each breath you are taking.

Now allow yourself… as you continue to grow this picture in your mind's eye… to tune into any

sounds that you can hear on this beach... Perhaps the distant sound of gulls... or the sound of a gentle breeze blowing... Perhaps the sound of the tide ebbing and flowing... back and forth... a gentle ebbing and flowing of the ocean... back and forth... so serene... the rhythm of the ocean... enhancing your feelings of calm and relaxation... enhancing your feelings of serenity.

Now... allow yourself some time... to look around... at anything else that you can see in this very beautiful place... Perhaps there are cliffs or mountains... that rise at the sides... perhaps there are trees or vegetation... Perhaps there are beautiful objects... stones and shells to examine and to explore... Perhaps there are boats at sea... that you can see bobbing... or moving gently, smoothly on the ocean.

Really allow yourself... time to explore this environment... As you do so... really allow yourself... to tune in to the beauty... and the tranquillity of the place... To feel it... to feel its essence... feel its sensations... Feel how relaxed... and peaceful this place is... and feel how relaxed... and peaceful... you feel in this place... The more time you spend.

Use all your senses... to truly experience... the peacefulness of the place... and as you do so...

you feel a wonderful sense... of deep relaxation... and calmness... This deep relaxation... is so powerful that it is growing stronger... and stronger... as each moment goes by... With it comes a deep sense... of confidence... and calmness... that is growing stronger... and stronger now... with each breath you take... This confidence... and this calmness... will remain long after this relaxation session... This confidence and calmness... will grow stronger and stronger within you... as each moment goes by... Day after day... moment after moment... week after week... this confidence and calmness... increasing in strength... and in depth... moment by moment... You feel so good... so strong... so joyful... and so confident... No matter where you are... no matter what you are doing... no matter whom you are with... Feeling confident and calm... day after day... stronger and stronger.

Now... as you grow the picture of this lovely environment... this lovely beach... allow yourself... to focus in on one aspect of it... and allow yourself to notice... what it is about this aspect... that is so lovely... so wonderful... Perhaps you would like to focus today... on the movement of the sea... or perhaps the brightness of the sky... Whatever you decide to focus on...

you are noticing now what it is... about this aspect... that is so wonderful and so beautiful... and so powerful... As you notice this... and as you recognise this... you are noticing this quality within yourself... You are feeling now... within yourself... your own strength... or beauty... or rhythm... or brightness... whatever that quality is... that you are noticing in the one aspect of this beautiful environment... Each time you listen to these words... you can focus on different aspects... or the same aspect... The choice is yours... Always you will be able to notice... and tune into that truly wonderful positive aspect... and to feel... to feel deeply within you... how that positive aspect relates to you... To feel your own sense of serenity... your own sense of beauty... your own sense of power... your own sense of purpose... your own sense of connection to everything else... or whatever else you are feeling in this moment... as you feel connected to that one aspect of this lovely place.

As you are doing so... you grow within you a wonderful feeling... of calmness... and serenity... as each moment goes by... and in turn... you grow within you strong sensations... of confidence... and calmness... that stay with you as each day goes by.

Now… as you listen to these words… allow yourself a few more moments… of deep relaxation in this very special place.

Now… slowly, gradually… allow yourself to let the image and experience of this lovely, beautiful place… just fade within your memory… so that you can remember it for another time… when you are relaxing once more… As the lovely beach fades into your memory… you notice that the lovely feelings that you are experiencing… are staying with you… so that when you have finished listening to these words… you will still be feeling confident… calm… and joyful… for a long time after.

Rest for a few more moments… Take your time now… becoming aware that you have been in deep relaxation and giving yourself time to orient yourself back to your own environment… In a few moments' time… I shall count to three and as I count… you will become fully awake and fully alert and completely ready to carry on your day… Then I shall tell you to open your eyes and you will open your eyes and be ready to carry on your day feeling alert and awake and calm and confident. As you continue listening to these words you know now that the time is coming very quickly now when you are ready

GENERAL RELAXATION AND CONFIDENCE SCRIPT

to open your eyes and be fully awake once
more, fully back to full conscious awareness
now. Beginning to count now... one... two...
and three knowing now that you are fully wide
awake and open your eyes.'

97

Chapter 10

Thinking in the positive

What is the difference between telling yourself 'I will pass' or 'I won't fail'? Telling yourself the first statement is more likely to help you pass your driving test. Think about the second statement for a moment. What is the one word that rings on in that sentence? It is the word 'fail.'

The way you structure your sentences, whether you are saying them aloud to others or saying them to yourself, has a strong effect on the way you do things. We often subconsciously use negative statements in conversation such as 'I'm not feeling too anxious', which simply makes us feel more anxious.

EXERCISE

Today, keep a notebook with you and jot down every negative statement that you hear yourself saying, or that you hear someone else saying to you. You may be surprised at how many there are. Here are some common ones:

'How are you feeling today?''Not bad.'

'Mind you don't drop that.'

'Don't stay out too long.'

You might be surprised to learn that your brain doesn't process negatives very well.
    Emotionally, what your brain hears is:

'How are you feeling today?'' – bad.'

' – drop that.'

' – stay out too long.'

w change the above statements into
actual positives:

'How are you feeling today?' 'Very well.'

'Hold that carefully.'

'Come back early.'

////////////////

The difference might seem subtle, but subtle can create big changes in our thinking and anxiety levels.

Sometimes, we even reinforce our negative statements with phrases such as:

'It's **bound** to all go wrong for me.'

'I **never** could do that.'

If you are telling yourself things like this, ask yourself, what is the evidence to suggest this? Is it really the case that you could never do something, or that it is bound to go wrong? You are creating negative self-suggestions when you talk in this way. Be kinder and gentler with your language:

'I don't know how it's going to go, actually, perhaps really well.'

'I haven't tried to do that but I expect I could.'

Are you using negative statements for gain?

Sometimes we use negative statements to gain reassurance and encouragement from others. We say, 'I know I'll fail' in the hope that our husband, mother or girlfriend will reply, 'Oh, don't be silly, of course you won't.'

The more forceful we become in our negativity, the more we convince ourselves that we cannot do something in our vain attempts to get praise or encouragement from the other person.

What is the point of doing this? The person you are complaining to will not be able to help you pass on the day. Only you can pass your test. Forget this game as it's unhelpful to you.

When the negative statements come from others

> **TIP**
>
> Switch off to people who joke at your expense about your skills. Usually this is due to their own insecurities.

Sometimes negative statements are not your own, but are from others around you; a competitive brother or sister, or an acquaintance who doesn't want you to succeed at something. Why not? Whatever reason they have, it is their own problem, not yours. Here is where you can really put your positive statements to good use. If anyone tells you 'you'll never pass', then tell yourself quietly and confidently that you will. You know you will pass because you are good enough and you want to pass.

Sometimes people around us don't realise they're being so negative, or that this might be affecting you, particularly if they are light-hearted about it.

Often a gentle reminder that they're being critical can be enough to put a stop to this. If someone is joking that you 'will never pass', then ask them quietly and seriously why they want or need to damage your chances of passing with such discouragement.

It is important for you to do this quietly and calmly otherwise it could lead to arguments, which are not going to be helpful to you.

Give yourself some strong positive affirmations

Positive affirmations feel very different to negative statements. Positive affirmations make you feel good and increase your confidence. Increased confidence makes you do things better. Make yourself a nice long list of positive affirmations, both general and specific to your driving test. Here are some to help you:

'I can and I will pass my driving test.'

'I am a good driver.'

'I am a good driver and every day I become a better driver.'

'I spend my time and energy on worthwhile things.'

'I am as capable as any other person of passing my test.'

'I am already good at (cycling/swimming/ cooking) so I know I am good at things.'

'There was a time when I could not (cycle/ swim/cook) but I learned really easily.'

'I am doing everything right to pass my test.'

'I am looking forward to being a driver.'

Here is the type of statement to keep off your list:

'I could be a good driver if I could do three-point turns.'

'I will be a good driver soon.'

'When I do more exercise, I will lose weight.'

Do not complicate them by adding conditions, as in the first statement, or by putting them in the future as in the other two. You are a good driver now.

Are your statements reflecting your acceptance of the challenge?

Are your statements littered with the word 'try'?

'I'll try my hardest to do the reverse manoeuvre properly.'

'I will try and do well.'

The word 'try' weakens your intention. Taken out, those statements become:

'I will do the reverse manoeuvre properly.'

'I will do well.'

These are more powerful statements – when an Olympic athlete prepares for a race, or a Premier League football player prepares for a game, there is no saying 'I'll try to win', only 'I will win.'

Pick the best of your positive affirmations and keep them regularly in your mind. Write them down for yourself in a place that you often see – perhaps on a Post-it on your mirror, or on different days in your diary.

What you tell yourself regularly becomes a reality much more easily. Forget any negative statements, and start thinking and talking in the positive. Practise this generally. Ban such replies as 'not bad' when someone asks you how you are, and change your reply to a nice, positive 'very well, thanks'.

Chapter 11

Other confidence and calmness building methods

In this chapter, I am going to give you tools and methods that you can use on the day of your test. Take time to set up and practise the methods that I describe. Knowing that you have these tools will enhance your confidence.

Breathing calm

> **TIP**
>
> Regulating your breathing will regulate other bodily processes, like your heart rate and blood pressure.

This method is a simple relaxation tool th
of us use all the time anyway, either cons
or not. Although it's simple, I advise that
have a history of breathing problems, then chat
to your doctor before practising any breathing
exercises.

Our breathing changes depending on whether
we are calm or anxious; and our breathing is
something that we can consciously control even
though it is usually under our subconscious
control.

Many anxious people actually over-breathe.
This means that they take in too much oxygen,
either by breathing too fast or by taking big
breaths in.

Reversing this consciously means we can
breathe ourselves calm.

EXERCISE

Anxiety is the polar opposite to relaxation. By
simply breathing slower and breathing out
for longer, we can help ourselves relax.

Take a short breath in and then release it in
a nice, long sigh, breathing in through your

nose and out through your mouth, letting the air whoosh through your teeth and lips. Do this a few times and you will feel more relaxed.

Now enhance the relaxing effect by setting yourself a word that you say through your mind when you breathe out. I suggest a word such as 'calm'.

Try this now. Take a gentle breath in, and then breathe out for longer through your mouth and at the same time say the word 'calm' through your mind.

As you do this, you are calming yourself by regulating the amount of oxygen in your body and allowing those overactive physical processes a chance to relax.

Before or during your test, you can take a few moments to do this exercise to promote your feeling of calm.

Extended breathing

Here is a more formalised breathing exercise that you might like to try.

Anchors are based on principles of neurolinguistic programming (NLP), a particular branch of hypnotherapy, and will be very helpful to you on your driving test.

Read this section carefully and take the time to set up a nice strong anchor for yourself. Once set, you will strengthen it without even thinking about it each time you have a driving lesson, and it will automatically be in place when you take your driving test.

The anchor is so called because you anchor a positive feeling with something else – in this case, an action and a word. Then, each time you use the action and the word, the feeling happens automatically.

Many professional sportspeople, actors, presenters and speakers use NLP anchors. Set your anchor well and it will serve you whenever you need it.

///////////////////////////

EXERCISE

Sit comfortably and relax for a few moments. Concentrate on feelings of confidence, calmness and control. To help yourself,

remember a time when you felt these feelings and remind yourself how the feelings felt at the time.

Now, follow this procedure carefully:

a) Allow a word to come into your mind that signifies or describes this feeling for you; it can be any nice, positive word. Here are some examples that my clients have given:

Calm – perfectly describes the state of calm.
Yellow – where yellow describes the colour of control and confidence.
Sienna – place visited where I felt the most calm and relaxed.
Lucy – name of pet dog that I have shared such happy, relaxed times with.

You need one word to link with this good positive feeling.

b) Now you need an action. A nice, easy, private action that does not interfere with what you are doing at the time.

As this anchor is for your driving, I suggest you use holding the steering wheel. After all,

you will be holding the steering wheel for most of your driving test. A short tightening of your grip on the wheel at any time will further strengthen your anchor. Not only is this unnoticeable to your examiner, but it is easy for you to do.

c) Now you are going to link those nice, positive feelings with your special word and your special action.

Staying relaxed, focus on feeling calm, confident and in control. Really experience these feelings, enhancing them as powerfully as you can.

Use whatever resources you need to do this. Imagine that you are breathing the feelings in, or think of a time when you felt the same way; perhaps the time that you scored a goal for your team, or received praise from someone you admire.

Really concentrate on these feelings, so that you feel them all over your body, until they are as strong as they can be.

d) As soon as you reach this point of maximum strength, you can set your anchor. You do this by simultaneously saying your special word

through your mind and imagining that you are gripping the steering wheel of the car.

Do this now, enhance the feelings to maximum strength, and at that point say the word over in your mind and imagine gripping the steering wheel. Hold it for a few seconds and then relax.

e) Repeat actions c) and d) five or six times. This is vital to set the anchor.

Allow yourself to relax. What you have done is to set up a very powerful association between those feelings, actions and thoughts. The more you use your anchor, the stronger it will become.

For you, the true value of the anchor is that it works the other way around. Want to immediately feel calm, confident and in control? Simply grip the steering wheel and say your special word through your mind. The feelings will happen automatically.

When you are taking your driving lessons, get into the habit of saying your special word through your mind as you take hold of the steering wheel. Each time you do this, your anchor will become stronger.

Your anchor is now a tool that you
with you on your driving test. Use it
you start, and use it during your test ar,
you need extra feelings of confidence, calm
and of being in control.

Dealing with mistakes

If everything is going fine on your driving test and
you then make a mistake, it is important that you
put it out of your mind and carry on. You know
that you are allowed to make a mistake or two on
the test, so being able to drive well after a mistake
will mean that you can still pass the test.

On my first driving test, I made a mistake and
then could not put it out of my mind. The mistake
was not the failure; it was my attention wandering
back to it so that I was not concentrating on what
I was doing.

Letting a mistake go is a two-part process.
First, you put the mistake out of your mind, and
then you get back to full concentration. Here
is an exercise to help you to do this. Practise this
exercise by using it while you are taking your
driving lessons.

EXERCISE

If you make a mistake, follow this procedure:

Step one
a) Bring to mind an image of a piece of paper. Now, transmit the mistake onto the piece of paper. You can imagine this as a word or picture on the paper or any other way that works for you.

b) Now, imagine that you are crumpling the paper into a tight ball with the mistake inside it.

c) Throw the ball of paper away in your imagination. As it goes, it takes the mistake with it. As you do so, let your mind know that thinking about and feeling that mistake are over.

Do not take too long over this – a second or two is all you need – and do it at an appropriate moment. Through practice, you will make this an almost subconscious process.

Practise it now. Think back to a mistake you made recently. Quickly visualise a representation of that mistake being crumpled in the paper and thrown away.

Step two
Now use the anchor that you set for yourself earlier in this chapter. Take a nice steady breath outwards, grip the steering wheel tightly and say your word through your mind. Now you are feeling confident, calm and in control once more, you are ready to carry on driving well.

Practise these exercises until they are perfect for you. You may not even need to use them on your driving test, but knowing that you have these tools will increase your feeling of being in control, and being calm and confident.

Chapter 12

Putting it all together

Well done for reaching the final chapter of this book. By now you will be feeling better about your driving. This chapter is to remind you of what a good position you are now in to take your driving test. It is a good idea to read this chapter again just before you take your test, so make a mental note to do this.

As your test day arrives, remember all the preparation that you have been doing:

✓ You have taken a good course of driving lessons.

✓ You have learned all the skills that you need to pass the test.

✓ You are driving at a level that your instructor knows is good enough to pass your test.

✓ You have put in extra practice as required.

✓ You have taken care of yourself and you feel fit and strong.

✓ You have practised the exercises in this book.

✓ You have been listening to the recording of the script regularly.

✓ You have visualised yourself taking and passing your test many times.

✓ You are feeling relaxed, calm, confident and focused.

Your driving instructor knows that you are a good driver. They are confident that you will pass your driving test; otherwise, they would not have advised you to take it. They may have taught hundreds, perhaps thousands of new drivers, and they know what level of competence you need to pass a driving test.

Moreover, remember that a professional instructor's reputation is based on their pass rate, so it is to their advantage to know that you are ready before advising you to apply.

Positive visualisation

You feel ready and you feel good. Now do some nice, positive visualisation so that you feel even better.

While you have been playing your driving test script, you have been nurturing your powers of relaxation and visualisation.

Positive visualisation is one of the strongest motivating forces that we have, so use it now. Below is a brief exercise for you. Read it through first, and then practise it.

EXERCISE

Sit or lie down somewhere comfortable where you will be undisturbed for a few minutes, and close your eyes.

Imagine that you are driving some time in the future after you have passed your test. You are driving in a beautiful place, and you are driving a really great car.

Perhaps a classic Mercedes through a stunning European landscape, or a convertible along

Route 66 in America. Let your imagination take you to your best driving experience.

Let your imagination run wild for a while and get really involved in this idea. Perhaps there is great music playing on the car stereo, so allow yourself to hear that music.

Imagine how good you would be feeling; exhilarated and inwardly relaxed at the same time. Feel how responsive the car is, and how naturally you are driving.

Grow this feeling, as you grow this picture in your mind. Grow the brightness and colour of this picture, as if you were turning up the controls on a TV screen. Grow the picture larger. Turn the volume up on the sounds in this little daydream; take this as far as you want to.

As soon as your test is passed, driving can and will feel just as joyful as you are imagining now. You are in this moment, experiencing the joy of your driving.

Now, rewind time in this little movie in your mind. See yourself first as a driver, driving your car. Going to places you want and when you want to go there. Feel your sense of freedom.

Rewind time a little more and see yourself now passing your driving test. See, hear and

feel yourself at the moment you are told that you have passed. Allow this picture to grow bright, bold and strong. See how pleased you are, feel how happy you are. This is happening to you. This is what will happen to you.

Keep with this exercise for as long as you want to and then in your own time allow yourself to open your eyes again. Now keep these good feelings with you throughout the rest of the day.

The day of the test

You wake up and you realise that today is the day. You feel excited and you feel good. Spend a few moments just relaxing before you start your day. You have, of course, given yourself plenty of time to get ready, so there is no rush.

Eat something good for breakfast. This is important. Food will help you to feel balanced and grounded and you feel calmer when you have a good meal inside you. Eat slowly so that you can digest your food properly.

Make sure that you have had plenty of fluids to drink. You do want to be properly hydrated, particularly if it is a warm day, so that you will be as balanced and as grounded as possible.

Tea, coffee and cigarettes all have the effect of stimulating you so avoid them if you can. If you cannot, then do not go overboard with them and choose decaffeinated drinks. If you are a smoker, you know that cigarettes do not relax you – in fact, they do the opposite. A few moments of breathing exercises will be more beneficial.

Dress in something that is comfortable and that makes you feel confident. Wear shoes that you have driven in before and that feel right for you when you are in the car. If you wear glasses to drive in, then remember to wear them now.

Make sure that you have all your documents with you – your driving licence, your theory test pass certificate – and you are all set. Take a deep breath and feel that sense of calm.

Your pre-test lesson

The pre-test lesson is not essential, but most driving instructors strongly recommend it and so do I. It gives you the opportunity to settle into your driving.

When you are in the car, ready to take your pre-test lesson and drive to the centre, remember to use your anchor to increase your calm, controlled and confident feelings. All the time that your hands are on the wheel, your calmness and confidence is growing stronger and stronger.

By the time you arrive at the test centre your confidence will be very strong and you will be feeling well relaxed and focused.

While you are waiting, you can practise your breathing exercises if you wish. When the examiner is ready, pay attention to what they are saying and if there is anything that you do not understand or find confusing, then ask for clarification. We feel much more settled when things are clear in our minds.

Your driving test

TIP

Trust yourself and your abilities. You have worked hard to reach this point and all your skills and knowledge are safely stored in your subconscious, ready to be utilised.

You have, with the help of the script in this book, already taken and passed your driving test many times in your own imagination. Each time you did this, you have been setting in your mind the firm belief, as far as your emotions are concerned, that you have already passed the test. Now you are ready to take and pass the test one more time.

Now in the car, your hands are on the wheel and once again you have that strong feeling of calm, confidence and control.

All the while that you are consciously focusing on your test, your subconscious is telling you that you are a good driver and that you can do this easily and comfortably. As this happens, you will find that your concentration is very strong. You will find that your practical skills are strong. You will find that the examiner finds the experience of being driven by you to be a pleasant one.

Follow the guidelines outlined in this book and you will greatly improve your chances of driving well, certainly well enough, with good instruction, to pass your driving test easily and confidently. Drive well and enjoy the day.

Conclusion

The skills you have gained while working with this book will greatly improve your chances of driving well. Now, when you have passed your test, you can look forward to being a relaxed, calm and confident driver. These skills will also help you in many other areas of your life. The key to feeling confident and inwardly calm is to recognise that you have all the resources you will ever need to do everything that you could ever want to do. When you recognise this, you find that anything that you set your mind to happens so much more easily for you.

When you have successfully mastered your anxiety levels, you will find that you sleep more easily, have more energy and more focus, and feel more at ease with everything you do.

The skills that you have been learning in this book can be utilised in so many other areas of your life. You can, if you wish, continue to use your general relaxation script for any time in your life when you feel that you need an extra boost of confidence or some deep relaxation time.

www.summersdale.com